# I Love to Draw!

Jennifer Lipsey

**LARK BOOKS**
A Division of Sterling Publishing Co., Inc.
New York

## My Very Favorite Art Book

This book is dedicated
to the kids at Veritas

**Editor**
JOE RHATIGAN

**Creative Director**
CELIA NARANJO

**Associate Art Director**
SHANNON YOKELEY

**Editorial Assistance**
DELORES GOSNELL

Library of Congress Cataloging-in-Publication Data

Lipsey, Jennifer.
  My very favorite art book : I love to draw / by Jennifer Lipsey.
     p. cm.
  Includes bibliographical references and index.
  ISBN 1-57990-629-X (hardcover)
  1. Drawing—Technique. I. Title.
NC730.L565 2005
741.2—dc22

                                         2005010716


10 9

Published by Lark Books, A Division of
Sterling Publishing Co., Inc.
387 Park Avenue South, New York, N.Y. 10016

© 2005, Jennifer Lipsey

Distributed in Canada by Sterling Publishing,
c/o Canadian Manda Group, 165 Dufferin Street
Toronto, Ontario, Canada M6K 3H6

Distributed in the United Kingdom by GMC Distribution Services,
Castle Place, 166 High Street, Lewes, East Sussex, England BN7 1XU

Distributed in Australia by Capricorn Link (Australia) Pty Ltd.
P.O. Box 704, Windsor, NSW 2756 Australia

If you have questions or comments about this book, please contact:
Lark Books
67 Broadway
Asheville, NC 28801
(828) 253-0467

Manufactured in China

ISBN 13: 978-1-57990-629-0
ISBN 10: 1-57990-629-X

For information about custom editions, special sales, premium and corporate purchases, please contact Sterling Special Sales Department at 800-805-5489 or specialsales@sterlingpub.com.

# CONTENTS

# Art is Awesome!

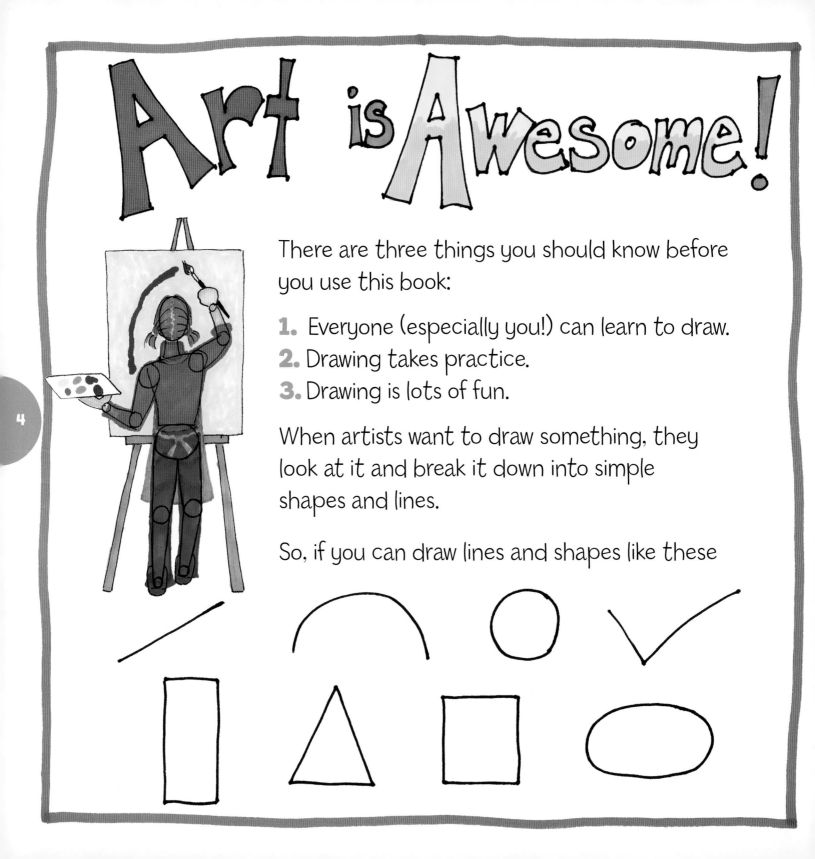

There are three things you should know before you use this book:

1. Everyone (especially you!) can learn to draw.
2. Drawing takes practice.
3. Drawing is lots of fun.

When artists want to draw something, they look at it and break it down into simple shapes and lines.

So, if you can draw lines and shapes like these

then, with some practice, you will be able to put them together in fun and different ways to draw things like these

Want to know more? Turn the page!

Drawing is something you can do almost anywhere.

You can draw in your  or in a

or at a  or even up a .

All you need to get started is a

and some

The drawings in this book are colored in with

but you can also use

or

The pages on the left side of this book show lots of cool instructions.

Each new step is shown in PINK. The steps already finished are in BLACK. Like this:

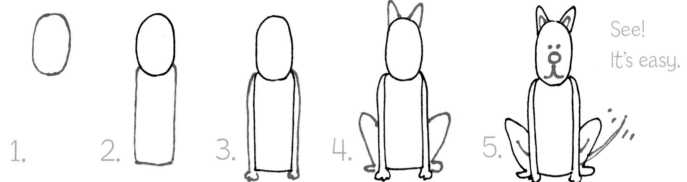

1.　　　2.　　　3.　　　4.　　　5.

See! It's easy.

Use a pencil to draw your objects. Draw lightly so it will be easy to erase any extra lines. Then, add color if you want.

The pages on the right side of the book show fun ways to use what you've learned.

# Underwater

## FISH

 1.      2.      3.     4.     5.     Add some stripes.

## BLOWFISH

 1.      2.      3.

### UNDERWATER PLANT

 1.      2.     3.

## CLOWN FISH

 1.      2.      3.     4.

## SHARK

 1.     2.     3.     4.     Erase the extra lines.

8

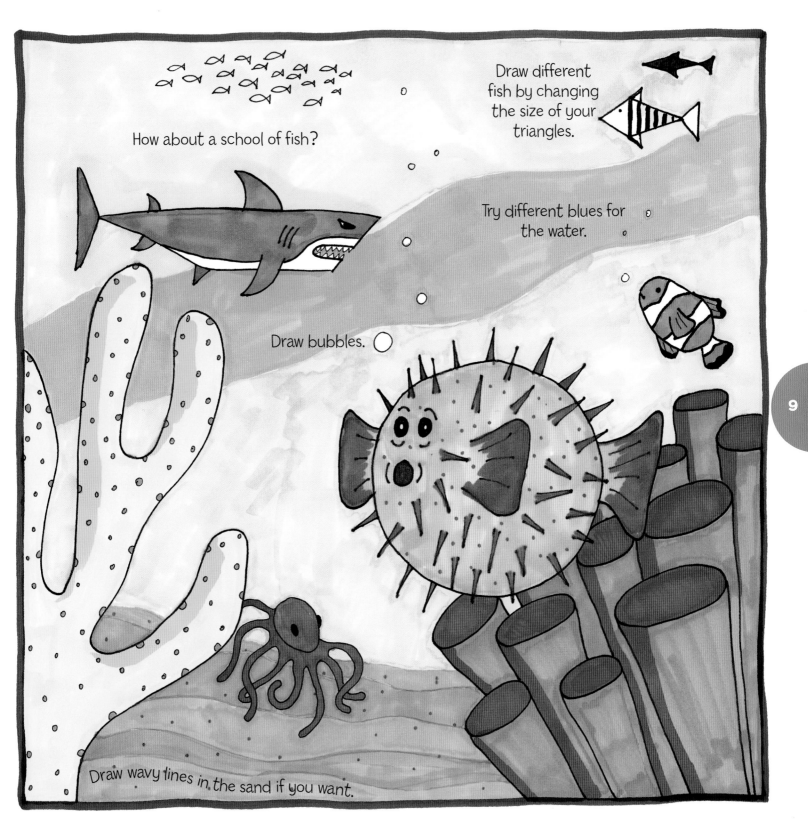

How about a school of fish?

Draw different fish by changing the size of your triangles.

Try different blues for the water.

Draw bubbles.

Draw wavy lines in the sand if you want.

9

# Bugs

## CATERPILLAR

1.

2.

3.

## BUTTERFLY

1.

2.

3.

### OVERLAPPING GRASS

## SNAIL

1.

2.

3.

### LADYBUG

1.

1.

2.

2.

## SPIDER

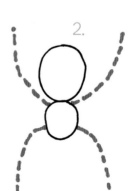

1.

2.

3.

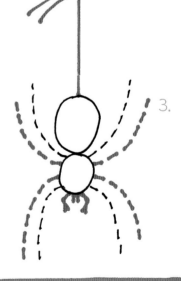

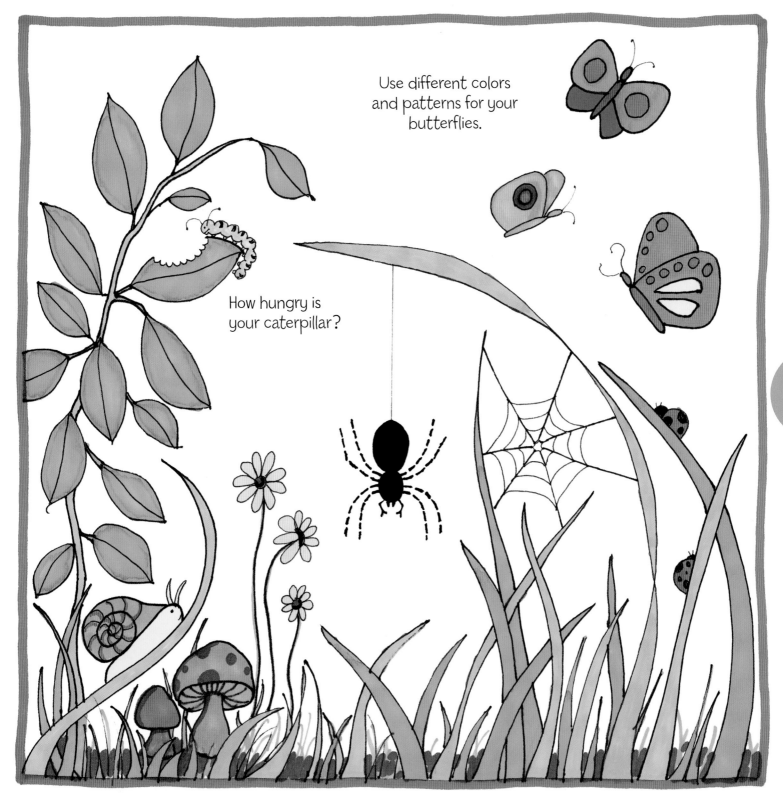

Use different colors and patterns for your butterflies.

How hungry is your caterpillar?

11

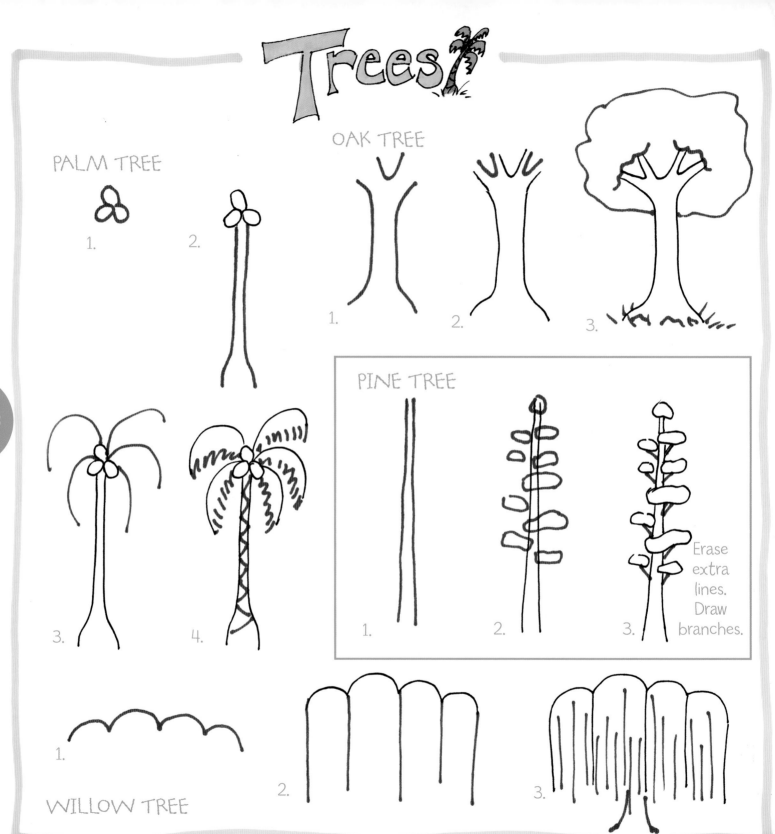

# Trees!

## PALM TREE

1.

2.

3.

4.

## OAK TREE

1.

2.

3.

## PINE TREE

1.

2.

3.

Erase extra lines. Draw branches.

## WILLOW TREE

1.

2.

3.

Draw curved lines to show the wind blowing.

Try different greens and yellows for your tree.

Want to draw hills? See page 20.

How about a swing?

Add more branches.

See page 44 to draw trucks and cars.

Draw yellow lines under the sun for a sunset.

13

# Flowers

## DAISY

1.

2.

3.

4.

5.

## TULIP

1.

2.

3.

4.

## ROSE

1.

2.

3.

4.

5.

## FLOWER IN A VASE

## SUNFLOWER

Turn your paper as you draw the petals.

1.

2.

3.

Things drawn small at the top of your page look far away.

Want to draw a barn? See page 23.

Things drawn big at the bottom of the page look close up.

# Sweets

## ICE CREAM CONE

 1.  2.  3.  4.

Don't forget the cherry on top!

Add more scoops!

## HARD CANDY

 1.  2. 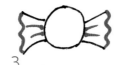 3.

## CUPCAKE

 1.  2.

 3.  4.

Add frosting and sprinkles. Yum!

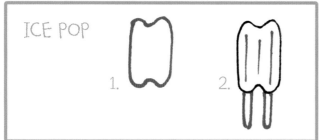

ICE POP 1. 2.

## BIRTHDAY CAKE

 1.  2.  3.

Blow out the candles.

## CHOCOLATE CHIP COOKIE

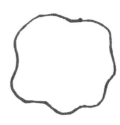 

16

 **Winter**

## SNOWMAN

1.

2.

The first snowball overlaps the second one.

3.

4.

Now decorate! Don't forget the hat.

## CHRISTMAS TREE

1.

It's good if your branches look different.

2.

Don't forget the trunk.

3.

Draw one line under the trunk and another one behind the trunk for snow. Add more branches, and decorate!

### HOLLY BERRIES

1.

2.

3.

## CANDY CANE

## SNOWFLAKE

1.

2.

3.

4.

Try different snowflake designs.

How about a snowlady?

Turn to page 26 to draw cool boxes.

19

# Mountains

## HILLS

1.

2.

3.

## MOUNTAINS

1.

2.

3.

Add as many
mountains as you want.

## SNOWY MOUNTAINS

1.

2.

3.

## VOLCANO

1.

2.

3.

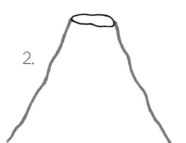

Draw rocks
and lava.

# Buildings

## HOUSE

Add the windows.

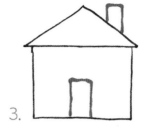

1.    2.    3.    4.

## CHURCH

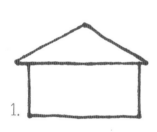

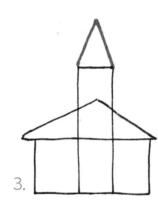

1.    2.    3.    4.

Erase extra lines and
add a door and windows.

## CASTLE

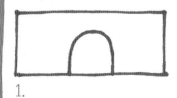

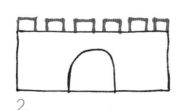

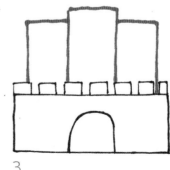

1.    2.    3.    4.

BARN

1.

2.

3.

4. Add a silo, doors, and a window.

What animals live on your farm?

# The Big City

**1.** Start like this.

**2.** Now keep drawing without lifting your pencil from the paper.

Now add lots of details, such as windows, chimneys, domes, towers, and steeples.

**3.**

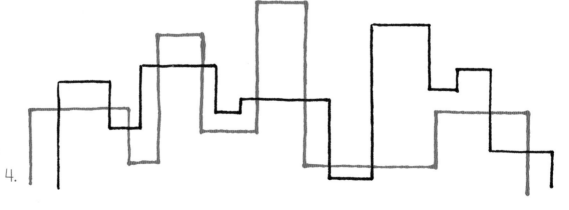

Now try drawing another city line that overlaps the first one. Erase extra lines.

**4.**

24

MORNING

Use more than one sky color.

Color around the sun to leave it white.

DAY

Leave white in the sky to show clouds.

NIGHT

When coloring the sky, leave tiny bits of white for the stars.

To make a whole building look lit up, color the yellow in first, and then draw thick black lines on top for windows.

# 3-D Objects

## CUBE

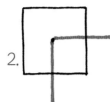

1. Draw a square with a dot in the middle.

2. Draw another square on top of the first one, starting from the dot.

3. Connect the four corners.

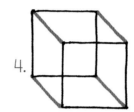

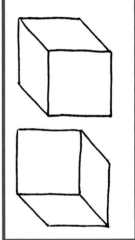

Erase lines to make the cube look solid.

## CONE

1. Draw an oval.

2. Center a dot above the oval.

3. Connect the dot to the sides of the oval.

## CYLINDER

1. Draw an oval.

2. Draw another above the first.

3. Connect the sides with straight lines.

## 3-D ROAD

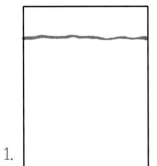

1. Draw a line toward the top of your paper.

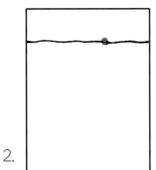

2. Put a dot on the line.

3. Draw a triangle down from the line.

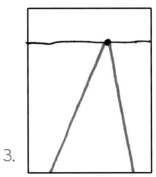

4. Draw a dotted line down the middle.

26

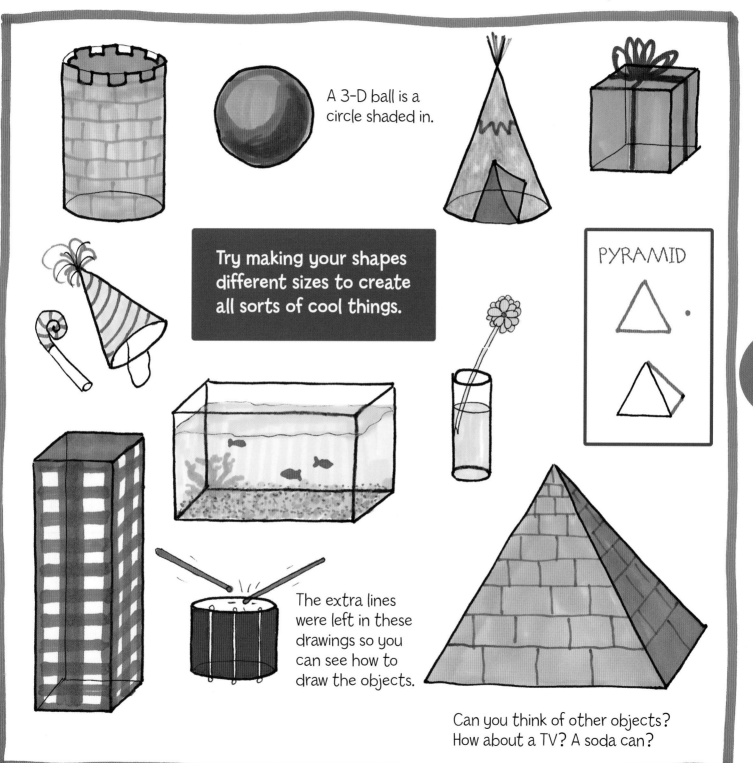

A 3-D ball is a circle shaded in.

Try making your shapes different sizes to create all sorts of cool things.

PYRAMID

The extra lines were left in these drawings so you can see how to draw the objects.

Can you think of other objects? How about a TV? A soda can?

# Dogs & Cats

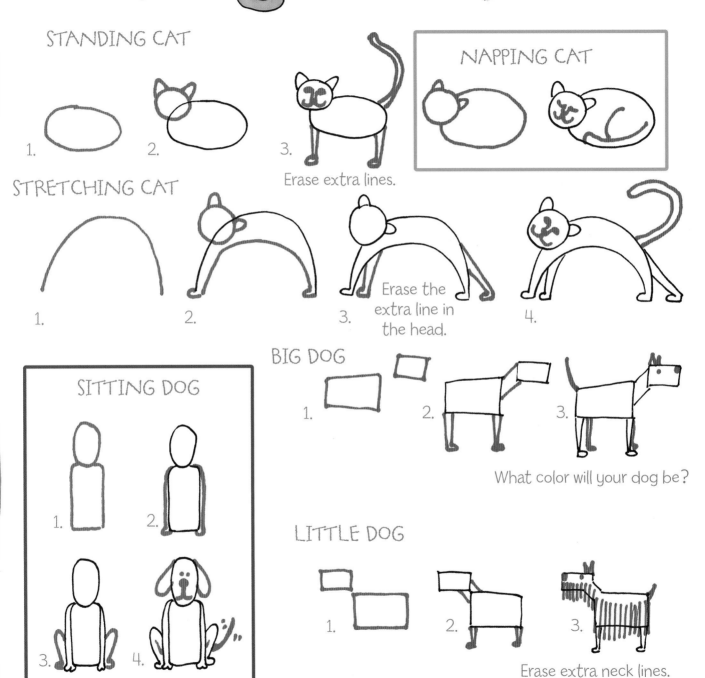

STANDING CAT

1.  2.  3.

Erase extra lines.

NAPPING CAT

STRETCHING CAT

1.  2.  3. Erase the extra line in the head.  4.

BIG DOG

1.  2.  3.

What color will your dog be?

SITTING DOG

1.  2.  3.  4.

LITTLE DOG

1.  2.  3.

Erase extra neck lines.
Add details and shaggy hair.

Try floppy ears.

Does your kitty like to look out the window?

Go to page 12 for more trees.

Try pointy ears.

Draw the hair sticking up on a stretching cat to make it a scared cat.

Check out the people on page 38!

# Birds

## PENGUIN

1.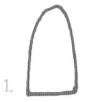
2.
3.
4.

## TROPICAL FLOWER

1.
2.
3.

## FLAMINGO

1.
2.
3.
4.

## TOUCAN

1.
2.
3.
4.

## CHICK

Add tiny lines to make it fuzzy.

## HEN

1.
2.
3.

## BARN OWL

1.
2.
3.
4.

Make up your own silly bird.

# Animals

## PIG

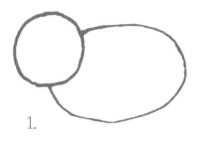

1.

2.

3.

## FROG

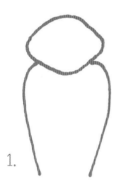

1.

2.

3.

## MONKEY

1.

Draw the arm and leg joints.

2.

See the people on page 38 for help.

Connect the arms and legs.

3.

Erase extra lines.

Add details.

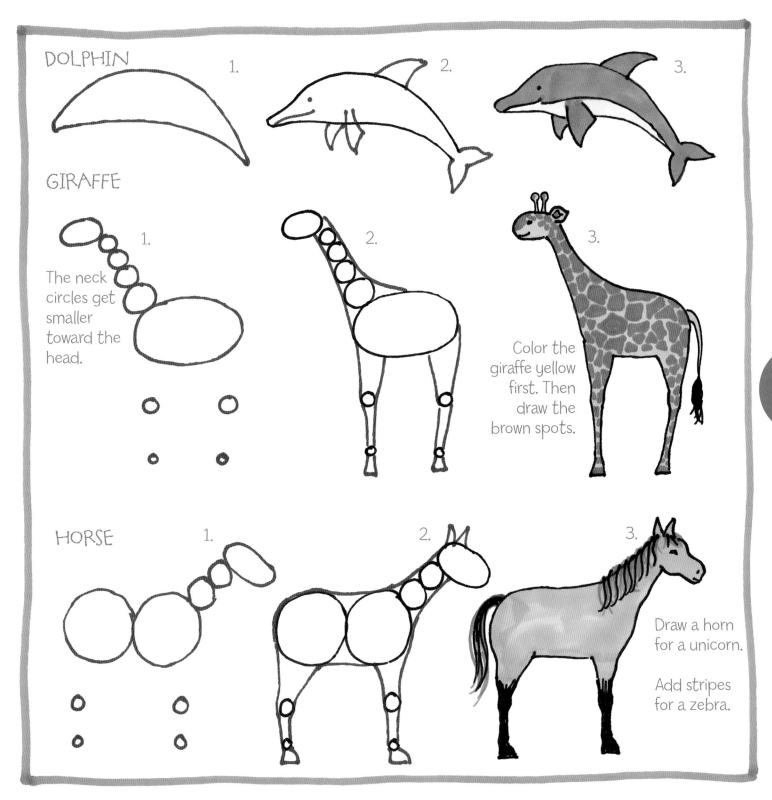

DOLPHIN
1.
2.
3.

GIRAFFE
1.

The neck circles get smaller toward the head.

2.

3.

Color the giraffe yellow first. Then draw the brown spots.

33

HORSE
1.
2.
3.

Draw a horn for a unicorn.

Add stripes for a zebra.

## APATOSAURUS

1.

2.

Add on six more circles and an oval for the head.

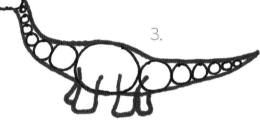

3.

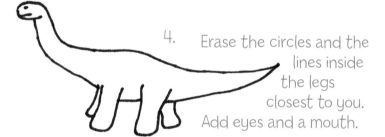

Draw a line around the body that touches all the circles. Draw the legs.

4. Erase the circles and the lines inside the legs closest to you. Add eyes and a mouth.

## TRICERATOPS

1.

Leave a small space between the head and the body.

2.

3.

Draw the horns and mouth.

4.

Erase extra lines. Add more details.

34

STEGOSAURUS

Want to draw hills and volcanoes? See page 20.

Learn to draw palm trees. See page 12.

TYRANNOSAURUS REX

# Faces

1.

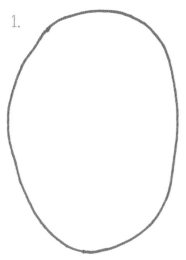

Draw an upside
down egg shape.

2.

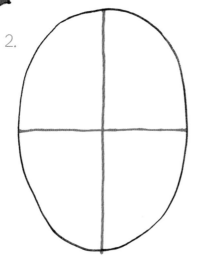

Divide it in half both ways.

3.

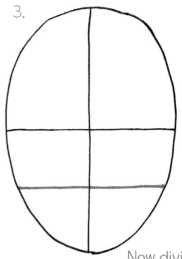

Now divide the
bottom half.

4.

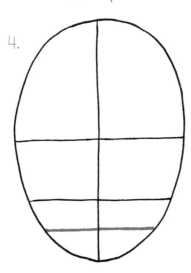

Do it again.

5.

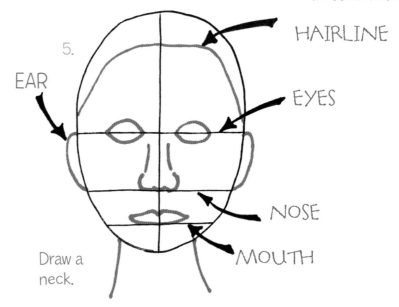

HAIRLINE

EAR

EYES

NOSE

MOUTH

Draw a
neck.

Now you know where all the
parts of the face belong.

Erase the lines after you
draw all the features.

Try different skin colors.

Don't forget eyelids and eyebrows.

Draw different hairstyles and colors.

How about a hat?

MAD

SURPRISED

SCARED

HAPPY

SAD

Look closely in the mirror and practice drawing your face. This is called a self-portrait.

SILLY

NAUGHTY

# People

## THE BODY

1.

Draw an oval head. Add the neck.

2.

Draw the torso.

3.

Draw an oval for the hips.

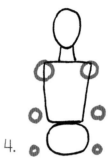

4.

Draw large circles that overlap the torso for shoulders.

Draw medium circles for the elbows and small circles for the wrists.

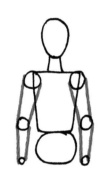

5.

Connect the circles to make arms. See how the arms get skinnier at the wrists?

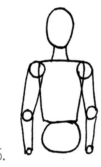

6.

Draw large circles for the knees and medium circles for the ankles.

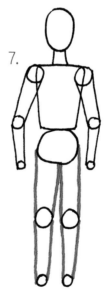

7.

Connect the circles to make legs.

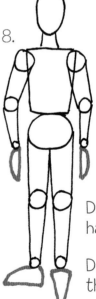

8.

Draw simple hands and feet.

Don't make them too small.

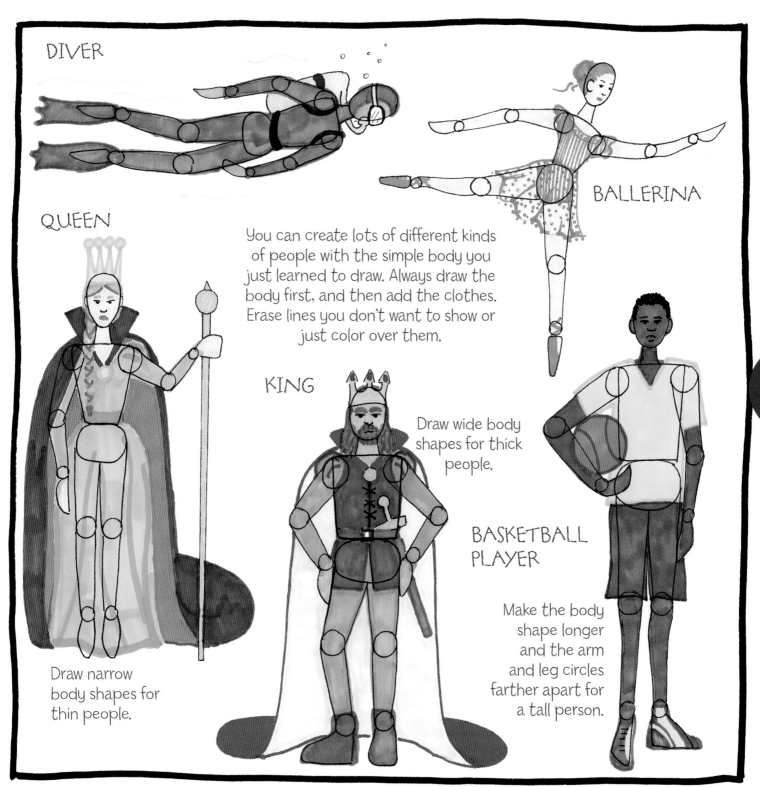

DIVER

BALLERINA

QUEEN

You can create lots of different kinds of people with the simple body you just learned to draw. Always draw the body first, and then add the clothes. Erase lines you don't want to show or just color over them.

KING

Draw wide body shapes for thick people.

BASKETBALL PLAYER

Make the body shape longer and the arm and leg circles farther apart for a tall person.

Draw narrow body shapes for thin people.

# More People

## SCIENTIST

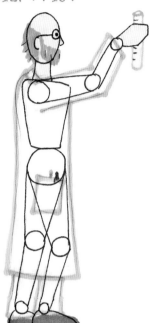

## SOCCER BALL

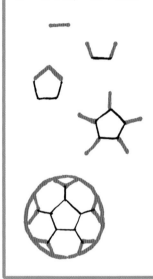

## YOUNG SOCCER PLAYER

Make the body shapes smaller and closer together for a little person.

## PIRATE

Make the shapes bigger and farther apart for a big person.

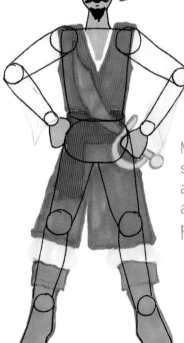

## MUSICIAN

Try tilting the head.

40

## PRINCESS

## FAIRY

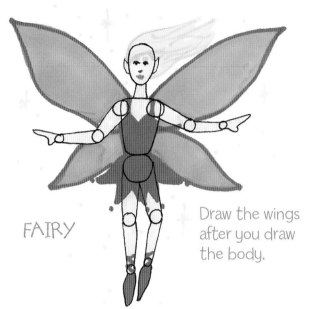

Draw the wings after you draw the body.

## WIZARD

Color the beard first, and then color the robe around the beard.

## YOUNG ARTIST

Try drawing a person from behind.

# Medieval Fantasy

## TROLL

1.

Draw the head, torso, and hips.

2.

Draw the arm and leg joints.

3.

Connect the circles to make arms and legs.

4.

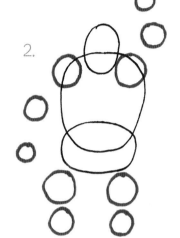

Erase extra lines and add feet, hands, and a face. Don't forget the club!

## DRAGON

1.

2.

Outline the body circles and draw legs.

3.

Add wings, teeth, spikes, scales, and horns.

See page 22 for castles.

KNIGHT

1.

2.

Add the arm and leg joints.

3.

Connect the joints. Add weapons and armor.

See page 39 for more Medieval people.

# Cars & Trucks

## SEMI-TRUCK

1.

2.

3.

## PICKUP TRUCK

1.

2.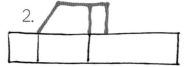

3.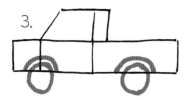

4.

Add windows, bumpers, and other details.

## SPORTS CAR

1.

2.

3.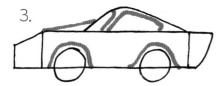

4.

Erase the extra lines, and add details.

## BEETLE

1.

2.

3.

4.

Draw a city.
See page 24.

Draw some parking meters.

# Wheels

## MOUNTAIN BIKE

1.

2.

3. Add a seat and handlebars.

4.

Draw the wheels.

5.

Add pedals, spokes, and tires.

## MOTORCYCLE

Draw the tire and wheel.

1.

Draw the fender, seat, and gas tank.

2.

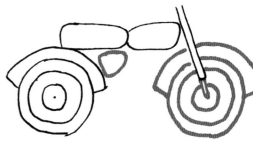

3. Add the front wheel and fender.

4.

Add handlebars, headlight, and exhaust pipe.

## SCOOTER

1.

2.

3.

Draw the tires.

4.

Erase extra lines. Add the seat, handlebars, and details.

See page 38 for people.

Draw skakeboards!

47

## Acknowledgments

I would like to thank God and all the great people in my life who have shared the value of beauty, creativity, and hard work with me. I am very grateful to my art teachers from elementary school to graduate school—you have made all the difference, and I am honored to have become a part of this important legacy.

Big thanks to Joe, my editor, for believing in the importance of this series and taking a chance on an abstract painter writing and illustrating children's books.

Thanks to my wonderful group of friends and family who have been so supportive and understanding all the times I couldn't hang out because of The Books. Extra big thanks to my husband, Martin, for so much love, trips to the art store, reading all the Harry Potter books to me while I worked, and the delicious sweet tea and home-cooked meals delivered to the studio.
I love you.

Special thanks to my young art students who didn't always know that they were the official project testers.
You're the greatest!

48

## Index

What do you want to draw?
Find it in this list and turn to the page listed next to it.